Star Messages

Codes to
Sing, Dance
and
Live by

Cheryl Lunar Wind
and Friends

Star Messages

Codes to Sing, Dance and Live by

Any Inquiries contact:

cheryl.hiller@yahoo.com

Some of the poems in this collection first appeared in

We Are One, Follow the White Rabbit, Know Your Way,

Love Your Light, Finding Our Way Home, We Are Light,

Handshake With the Divine chapbooks; and on facebook.

Front cover photo taken by a friend.

First edition.

Published by Alexander Agency Books, Mount Shasta, California 96067

ISBN 979-8-9897287-2-5

This book is dedicated to

Chief Golden Light Eagle
and
the Way of Respect for All life!

Preface

The Star Knowledge Reunion of 2017 was held in Gillette, Wyoming at what is commonly called Devil's Tower. Everything there was alive, the red hills had faces, and the trees and plants talked to us. It was a week long event, days of fasting, vision quests and tobacco tying (making prayer ties of colored cloth and tobacco).

We met in circle every evening. One special time, after drumming and singing native songs we connected with the great-Grandmother tree and received these messages:

She is sacred and so very powerful. The indigenous people lived in harmony with her and all life on Mother Earth. When visitors from other lands came they wanted to control the land and the people, after all, they saw it all as Resources to be used and had.

The huge Grandmother tree was cut down and sold to many places. More than greed, those men saw it as a way to disrupt the worship and harmony present between the people and the land. The huge tree was cut down and iron bands were placed on her stump to prevent her from regrowing. This also served to imprison her energies. The natives were disheartened by this blasphemy. They were then easier to control, and were forced to accept new ways of worship, inside little buildings. This was the message I received.

Many from that group circle also had messages to share. The Grandmother tree told us that her spirit was still alive, they were not able to kill her, but that she has been asleep, resting these many years until it was time to awaken. Her seven sisters in the heavens called out to her---also she heard our prayers during this time of vision quests and connection with the land spirits.

She told us that all trees on Earth are connected to each other, and no matter where we are when we leave her to go back to our homes we can touch any tree and talk to her.

Another sister present told us that the Grandmother tree is also a powerful portal. Walking around her base in one direction takes you back in time, and going in the opposite direction takes you into the future.

Also important to state is another way those men brought dishonor to her is when they named her Devil's Tower. She is a Sacred Earth Being and we returned honor to her by holding a renaming ceremony. From then forward she was to be called Celestial Tower or great-Grandmother. Attempts will also be made to have her name legally changed, like so many other sacred sites which were taken over and disrespected.

Grandmother's final message was a powerful one. Speaking for Mother Earth, she said the time for putting up with man's destruction is over. The destroying of the forests and all of their residents will not be tolerated anymore. Grandmother says Watch Out! It is time, I am taking my power back. We will see a cleansing and reordering. We have already seen what is called 'natural disasters', which many are a result of man's mismanagement.

The trees hold balance. This cutting down of my brothers and sisters must stop. Little humans need to learn respect.

Message from Holy Dove:
(A Review) This message shows the importance of Respect for all life.

"Know, O Peoples, that you must treat your *Relations of the Animal Nations* with great respect; for, they have held the balance when you did not even know such a thing."

"Know, O Peoples, that you must give your respect and honor to the *Plant and Tree Nations*; for they have fed you when you didn't even know you were hungry."

"Know, O Peoples, you must respect the *Stone and Mineral Nations* as well as the *Invisible Ones* that walk about; if it were not for their guidance most Two-leggeds would have fallen into their own traps and remained there."

---*The Symbols, The Universal Symbols and Laws of Creation: A Divine Plan by Which One Can Live*

<u>Many thanks to these contributors</u>:

Master Hilarion

Lauren Willow Fox

Mercy (Hawkwomyn) Talley

Cody Ray Richardson

Dave Harvey

Mikasa Tamara

Le'vell Zimmerman

Wolf Martinez

Snowflower Thorner

Alyssa Narum

Orason Orason

A'Marie B. Thomas-Brown

Darrel Johannes

Susan Grace

Shianna Freeman

Contents

We Are Them
by Cheryl

Avatars.
We are all Avatars.
We don this human form--
flesh body--
It is a vehicle.

We are the ones we have been waiting for.

Volunteers for this Earth mission.
Pleiadian, Andromedan, Sirian and
many other ET families---
--We Are Them.

Go within the heart door--
Swim in the cosmic ocean.
Play a game of star-tag.

Want to know of your origins;
Just ask.
Ask yourself.
The answers are within you.

We are light-extensions
of Source consciousness--
We are not lost, our steps
are deliberate--
There is a plan.

We are the ones we have been waiting for.

Man, Know Thy Self!
Message from Master Hilarion

"Think about the great Central Flame within the center

of your Being. Dwell upon it and allow it to expand

until you are in the middle of it, and it is all about you,

and in you. See what a Sun you have become! what

a Sun You Are! And this is the Pattern For All Creation.

Understand the Laws governing your own Light and

you will understand the Laws governing all Light. As

you become a Sun--as has every electron; for the

Consciousness, the Law, the Intelligent Electronic

Substance of the Great Central Sun, composes, animates

and causes to continue in its orderly operation and joyful

existence, all Creation."

---"I Am" The Open Door, 1978

Message for today from Arcturus...
Channeled by Lauren Willow Fox

Open to the light
The light is you
Solar star power
Starlight
Renew

Sunshine is you
Shadows dissolving
Earth revolving
All evolving
Held in glorious light

God is love
Christ Sun consciousness
Love is you
Hold each other
Sister and brother

Love Your Light
by Cheryl

The Sun is the heart
of all that is.

Our heart is a Sun--
shining, sparkling
lighting our path.

Only by Cheryl

corruption, greed, and ignorance---

Chemtrails--
Prescribed burns--
"thinning" of forests--

Every night, Gaia
and the land here grieve
the negative energies placed upon her---
She is saturated.
She calls for our help--

In the mourning--
the sun rises--
dissolving the last remnants
of the previous days atrocities---

Only
to begin again.

Grandfather Tree Park
by Cheryl

Some protect the forest, some fight fires---
Others call trees logs---
and take them away from their home.

Parks are safe places
from loggers and the Mill---
where people and trees
can be at peace.

My heart sits in awe--
of their unique beauty, firm resolve
and quiet strength.

4

Tree Knows
by Cody Ray Richardson

Tree knows
In it lives an advanced soul
It waves in the wind when pushed
Grows high once the wind is calm
It lightens its load of leaves when cold and hard
times come
It knows when to grow
It knows when to grow slow
It stands its ground no matter what unfolds
We see the trunk
We see the branches
We see the leaves
We see the seeds
Under it real nourishment hides
Away from all the challenges
Deep it holds
The subconscious
It provides for all
Until the day it falls

Spider's Message
by Cheryl

The rock, plant and animal kingdoms are family---
They exist peacefully.
They don't dig holes
to gather and collect---
to horde the gifts of Gaia.

Crystals are living beings---
talk to them---thank them.

Ever watch, The Lorax by Dr. Seuss---
everyone needs a thing-a-ma jig.
Not me---
"I speak for the trees."

Do like the Native Americans did,
take what you need and leave the rest.

I think the message from Grandmother Spider is---
Co-exist peacefully.
Respect all life.
Remember your ancestors.
If you come across a feather, rock or tree---
Ask the spirits before you take.
These things are sacred.
Don't use them for personal gain.
Take only what you need.
Talk to the rocks, trees and animals---
they are representatives of the Divine.

<----------------------------------->

Spiritual Law of Choice
(A Review)
Message from Bright Light-

"The Councils of Light are most eager to receive the *love* of human beings. For, human beings of Mother Earth will soon receive their admittance into the Galactic Councils through that awakening process known as *Full Consciousness.*"

"O Peoples of Mother Earth, it is more important that you should use this Spiritual Law to communicate with one another in a clear and loving way than for you to speak with the beings of Alpha Centari.

It is more important for the human being to learn to speak with the kingdoms of life on Mother Earth and the many realities within her body than to reach unto the Seventh Heaven and drink of its understandings.

It is more important for human being to utilize Spiritual Law of Choice to communicate with the inner worlds that are within their own Body, Heart and Mind than to reach into our Twin Universe Andromeda."

----The Symbols, The Universal Symbols and Laws of Creation: A Divine Plan by Which One Can Live

Before man can make contact with his Star families, he needs to master relationships here at home with his Earth families.

Mitakuye' Oyasin

Children of the Sun
by Cheryl

The god of ale
came to me and said
'take a whiff'
'have a sip'

You are a winner--
take a bow--
claim your prize--
a trip to the dome.

The dome shines, sparkles--
a golden Sun god.
Sura.

Children of the Sun---
Open your eyes
and see,
a secret message.

The Horizon---
holds the Key--
secrets lay
between the lines
spaces
ley lines--

Stepping
on earth grids,
We ignite the way
sparkle and shine
for all to see--
like a vein of gold
rising to the surface
hot lava
streaming---forging
new trails.

Cataclysmic Creation
by Cheryl

This explosive event is not the end all.
Earth shakes, quakes--

Woe, when mice weep.
Wink at the coming of the end of time.

Dine on your fear--
chew it up
spit it out.

Take it in stride--
Keep riding.
Be a 'Low Rider'.
Ride out the storm--
Big Bang.
'Riders of the Storm'
Thunderbirds.

Soar Free
like a flame--
Be the fire.

Lead.
Leaders lead.
Leaders of the pack.

Twins by Cheryl

Planets, alignments, squares.

Universes, galaxies, twin flames.

Dimensions, portals and planes of existence.

Andromeda and Milky Way are twin flame galaxies.

Do we have alternate versions of ourselves elsewhere?
The twins we never met?

Are there bird, feline and dolphins out there,
        like me?
Made of my stuff?

Can we fold time and space
and visit them?

Yes! We can.
We already do.
in our dreams.

T & T
by Cheryl

Tossin & Turning
means that your learning---

Going over the past---
Review.
Come back. OK
I'm here, now.

There's honor in letting go--

Area Codes
by Cheryl

Phone Home.

Earth	111
Moon	222
Sun	333
Arcturus	444
Sirius	666
Pleiades	777

Dial zero to get to Source.

Hop, Skip and Jump
by Cheryl

Will you jump on
--Stepping Stones--
Or
Skip like a rock
over still water?

---Hop, Skip and Jump--
(Time Jump)
It's not just for kids anymore.

There's a new game in town,
and we can all play.

Roll. Slide. Glide.

Be like a rock gliding over the water.
Rolling down the hill.
Rock and roll.

Adventurer; 3 poems
by Mercy (Hawkwomyn) Talley

And ~
Then there is flow
Where I Know
I'm fully protected
but not impeded
by rigidly set
parameters,
following inner
navigational fields ~
for Truth be known
I am an adventurer
who often sets sail
into uncharted domains

~ ~ ~

I develop
Substantiated
Trust to
Fuel my ship
Upon High Waters
Voyaging through
Seas rife with strife

~ ~ ~

There is a star
sparkling
on high
a planet perhaps
or a twinkling eye
reminding of
the grandeur sky...

hope sets sail
when looking
beyond,
glimpsing
the greater scale

~ ~ ~

14

Bird Tribes
by Mercy (Hawkwomyn) Talley
~ ~ ~

My poems are
Peaceful Prayers
I breathe upon
the wings
Of Doves
To Seed
The Bird Tribes
With Remembrance

~ ~ ~

Wind Inquiry
by Mercy (Hawkwomyn) Talley

I speak to
the harsh winds,
"what more
do you want
from me...?"

"only to make
you supple & resilient
in the hands of epic change"
is the reply

I can only respond
with a deep sigh ~

Naga
by Cody Ray Richardson

The truth like a knife
Cuts into reality
It makes me sick to live the way I do
Fantasy dressing in illusion
I'm not nice
I won't pretend to be anymore
Why should I believe anyone is
It's a twisted fate to be an internal soul in an impermanent world
Savage hungry ghosts rule here
To be to open is to be run over
To be to closed is to deny the lessons
How to be fair in a ruthless world
How to be protected yet still let others in
A old person with a dog
Sign of the time
A young person with a dog
The family is still strong
Just not a reality for some
Lucky and smart are those who walk the middle
Walk gentle and wield a big stick
In a land where dragons have taken on human form
We must form our own dragons
Naga protect me
Show me who is to help me
Who is to hurt me
I've had enough
It's a constant practice
Boundaries have to be clear
If they knew I was protecting them from me they would understand
They would not cross
Maybe I should tattoo my face
A true open heart must have a strong fist
A war chest
A brilliant pen
Friends who know
Character witnesses
Deep fake is real if you let it
I will not play telephone
Rumors stop with us
16

Is it true?
Did you witness it?
Is it good?
Wise words
Live by them or perish in the fire deception
Intention is everything
Deficiency and excess
Careful is the way
Brave wins the day
We all have two
Who I show you is up to you

Unicorn's Horn by Cheryl

You can call me Bareen---

We Unicorns don't use names in the sense that humans do.

We recognize each other by the feeling (wave and shine)
we get from each other.

We like the high up places on Earth,
mountains.

We also love the open fields
where we can run free
the wind caressing us.

Some of our colors are:
white, silver, pink, aqua and violet.

We are assigned a human to watch over---
they are those who live thru their heart---
the peaceful.

"The meek shall inherit the Earth."

We can use our horn
to pierce dark places---
to rescue our wards.

We are bold and kind.

Our song is celestial---
those with ears to hear,
listen for it.

Those who are aware---
see, feel and hear us.
18

Live in kindness.

Have compassion for the lost---
"They know not what they are doing."

We carry rainbow healing from our homes to yours.

We sometimes use humans
to deliver our message---
So,
Be careful
how you treat each other---
Lest you neglect
your healing.

Messages by Cheryl

Dark, night sounds find me,
Resting.

The ceiling fan, speeding along...
No where to go----
Always so insistent.

Finished Matrix 3 earlier.
Message received---CHOICE.
Been a theme lately.

The ringing in my head,
brings a peaceful knowing.
I am on the right path.

The Fortune Teller---
"I know because I must know.
It is my purpose. It's the reason I'm here,
the same reason we are all here."

Lemurian cards came in the mail today.
Message received---
'You express your divine will through sound;
words, tones and melodies.'

There will be harmony
between
Your humanity and your divinity.

Look up----to the sky.
Cosmic rays, orbs, sunbows, rainbows,
They are the divine delivery personnel.
Message received---
Be at peace.

A Pleiadian Passing By
through Dave Harvey

Feel to heal
A smile is hope
Create your own luck
Look for the new growth
Be patient in your rebirth
A recipe for peace dear one
---A Pleiadian passing by.

This Dragon Knows
through Dave Harvey

Nicira.
Angelic Dragon.
Tantric Ambassador to Gaia.
Gaelic in nature, at home in Avalon, at home in
Lemuria, at home throughout Andromeda.

The physical space you inhabit is a miracle,
your body is a miracle, and it is all powered by love.

This Dragon Knows.

Blue Ray Message
through Mikasa Tamara

Override density. Out of
compactness into your true
Identity.
Purity is Security. In every situation
Maintain High Vibration.
You are Divinity.
Source Proximity.
With miraculous Ability.
Infinite Capacity.
Love Dignity!

Your Consciousness is the
Obviousness! to your Full Power.
Getting you through Each Hour.
Because you know how to
Discern. Be Peaceful without
Concern. You are the Truth! So
you can sooth. Be the love Balm!
And Remain Calm!

All Is Well
by Le'Vell Zimmerman

Let it happen beloved.

The Light is steadily expanding here on the surface
of your world, where revelations are increasing
by the millisecond.

The more you ground yourself, the greater your
own sense of stability in existing beyond the
countless dramas continuously unfolding.

Beyond all preferences and opinions is the
absolute truth of eternal peace.

All Is well indeed.

#333

What is It?
by Wolf Martinez

It is not up there. Nor down there.
It is Right Here, All Around! In the Middle! In the Heart.
It is not in the dark, nor in the Light.
It is right in the Center, in between. It is Everywhere.
It IS in the absolute Stillness, in the Silence.
It is rapidly moving so fast you can barely see it if your not really paying attention.
It Sings a song that you can see in every color, so many Lights, So Bright.
See, if you look up, down, backward, forward,
all around with your Loving Human Heart, you will see It.
It is above, below, in the past, in the future,
right Here... Now, and All Around.
There is no place it is not,
but if you really want to see, hear, feel, and know It... Be still.
Listen to the sound between the breath. Humbly look Inside.
It will forgive you of all fear, anger, belief, and judgment
that you are willing to no longer be attached to because...
She Loves You SO Much.
She/ He... That which has no Gender is Everything. Everyone. Everywhere.
It is in YOU, not who you think you are.
What is It?

Hour Glass
by Cody Ray Richardson

It makes no difference
if it's the first or last grain of sand in the hour glass that drops
If unbroken all has its date
No one grain is more significant than the other at the time
Oh how twisted it is to borrow sand from other hour glasses
Breaking the glass in the process
Yet it is the way of this world
This world only being one world
To borrow from other hour glasses is to stay in the way of this world
Letting the sand fall naturally
is to know we are neither the sand nor the hour glass
This is to know the knowing of eternal life

Life Song*
by Snowflower Thorner

Misa, my Cherokee medicine womyn,
Taught me we are all born
with our own unique song

After six months' preparation,
she sent me to choose
a hill for my visionquest,
a song quest, actually

My task was to sit
quietly for four days,
three nights until my
Life song revealed itself.

So I sat, I watched
I waited. Not always
patiently. First night
forest exploded with
raucous, vibrating sound.

A sound deafening like
None I had ever heard
before. After long day
of meditating in place
I was tired.

Wishing noise to
end, I yelled loudly,
"Please stop now!"

To my complete and utter
shock, it did.

Next day, hummingbird
visited me three times.
Followed by dragonfly.

Finally, third day my
birth song emerged on
the ethers. So loud.
So clear.

Nourishing my spirit
unlike anything before
or since. I sang,
hummed it, desperate
to remember it...

To no avail. Hours later,
back in camp, the
song visit I waited
a year for had come
and gone

Like a
Vivid dream vanquished
By the brilliance
Of a new day.

*Inspired by a line in Robin Wall Kimmerer's book,
"Braiding Sweetgrass" where an indigenous guide says:
"Yes, I have learned the names of all the bushes, but I
have yet to learn their songs."

I Fly by Alyssa Narum

I fly with the wind, it shows me how to stay the course.

I dive into the sea, it shows me the beauty of ancient source.

Diyin nílíini bee it hodéezyééł sha nílééh.
(Holy God, you are the means of peace. To me, give it)

Hey yana, hey yana, hey yan yan

I burn with the fire, it melts away my fears into the dirt

I dig into the earth, its fertile soil nourishes the seeds of our rebirth

Diyin nílíini bee it hodéezyééł sha nílééh.

Hey yana, hey yana, hey yan yan

We celeberate this life it is a gift of ceaseless joy that we all share

We lift our hearts in love and know that heaven on earth is already
here

Diyin nílíini bee it hodéezyééł sha nílééh.

She who sings to the stars
knows her place,
no matter where her body resides
her soul is always home.
---Cheryl Lunar Wind

Lyran & Pleiadian Blessings
through Orason Orason

Zero Point....The energy changes, experiences change,
but consciousness itself does not change. Some call
this the quantum field. Others call this The Eternal Now
or the True Self. Unchangeable, always present under
everything. As you start to notice this field it comes
into the foreground (what is normally in the background).
Then it seems if you perceive dimensions that were not
there before. But this is not correct. They were already
there, you just didn't notice them. Because you observed
yourself through thinking. Now you are perceiving through
the sense of your feeling hearts.
----The Lyrans

If you have learned to focus, you have a skill that you can
apply in your future life, at all kinds of times, in all kinds of
situations. For example, focusing helps you find out what
you really feel and what you really want; you learn to deal
with self-criticism in a positive way. Focusing also helps you
release old pain and old patterns, or reintegrate those parts
of yourself that you have banished. This creates space for
inner growth and energy is released for new developments.
Focussing can benefit every other process you are working
on.
---The Pleiadians

Breathe
by A'Marie B. Thomas-Brown

Gaining lost ground in the silence that's so loud
The screams and moans releasing a buildup tension that seeks comfort
That seeks understanding
Comprehension even
Amid briars and thistles that conjugate among roses
Suppressing voice frequencies that I observe in unamused delight
For the sake of elevation
I'm facing
The hidden opposition
Amid my choosing to accept the unacceptable
Making peace with the argument abled
Understanding that it's always my ball
Always my court
I choose divorce in the name of Holy Matrimony
Aside from lost dichotomies
That scream
Peace
So I walk down the aisle
Aromatically
Decidedly
Choosing interruption
As a bridge to close the gap
Left gaping with the words
It's all good
Hearing the sound of every silent response
Creating space for me to respond
Or expand
Do you take Gratitude to be your energetic station
To have and to hold
From this exchange forward
As long as you shall live
I do
I now pronounce you here
Walk in the liberty that was created
Long before language attached to a sound
With the power to heal
To deliver
To set free
Every captive

That won't let you be
So breathe
And keep breathing
Until you see
That what you are looking for
You already have
And the shift
Has the power
To mend every rift
Elusively present
In the desert of my own conviction
Beyond trial and jury
Benched judgment
Verdict rendered
A heart tendered
In every I do
That leaves the door open
To further dialogue
Hope's initiation
The wine of evolution
Sipped at the appropriate time
On the hinges of the Eternal plow
I am well endowed
With every breath
In every frenetic frequency
Encountered
In stillness
So subtly
That it breaks the sound barrier
Transmuting love
Upward from the cliff
The precipice
As the movie credits role
My name in lights
Iridescent glow
I'm in the flow
Gotta go
Opened eyes see
It's all good
Breathe

Starchildren by Shianna Freeman

Crystal wolf spirit from Pleiades

Mother of the rainbow children

Sent to bring us to higher dimensions

Oh what a beautiful reflection

Eyes as deep as the ocean

A soul full of love and affection

Lyran starseed as wise as the white owl

Guiding us home in the night

The full moons are shining bright

Oh what a magikal beautiful light

A beacon for those who feel lost

A way home through the crashing waves

A light through these dark caves

A guide through the treacherous maze

Thank you starseeds for bringing me home

No longer I wander alone

Beautiful opportunities of growth you bring

A way through the mind

The beauty you sing

Raising earth's frequency

Deliberately transmuting energy

The wheels turn and my soul burns

With the fire of the sun and the stars

A burst of love straight from the heart.

My center I enter and the energetic spiral turns.

Experience by Cheryl

I am documenting these days---
the last of this collapsing system--
while we are moving into the new.

It's like an evacuation,
hurriedly running around
grabbing whatever
we might need to take.

Limited by time and space.
Even memories must be left behind.
Which ones do we save?

There are no mistakes--
it is learning.
Experience.

Alignment With True Nature
by Darrel Johannes

I can get to and am nearing a place,
where this world cannot hold me.

It has come through much pain and purging
of patterns very familiar and somewhat dear to me.

It has come through death. Not of the body, but of
things I learned that were not so. Things that did not see
my true nature, in spirit.

It's not words, idea or concept; not a lesson or abstract notion.
It's a Place. When this place is visited, seen and studied,
all will become very clear and self evident. It's how things
work when in Alignment With True Nature;
true life forces with love.
I will know It when I see It. It is my true home.

Move on Through
by Susan Grace

Life is on your side.
Oneness, Guidance, Consciousness Itself
Are always co-creating with you.

Your part is
Intention, Gratitude, Choices
That have you in your highest frequency.

You have to take responsibility for your own
Healing, Clearing and Centeredness
To meet Life at the Unfolding.

All is well.
You just have a pocket of density to move through.
You can do it.

Become Fully Conscious
by Le'Vell Zimmerman

Once again, no one can "make you feel" any type of way. You get to choose the emotional state you continue to entertain as a conscious being beloved.

Know that how you feel now is responsible for "what happens next" in your life and no one else's.

This is the power of emotional manipulation, where no one outside of you deserves to control how you feel right now.

You are not a "victim" here beloved.

The more you ground yourself, the more you take your power back beyond being susceptible to the constant manipulation and fearful programming of the external illusion.

You are not the constant fluctuations of the emotional body, but the peaceful stillness that observes and has the ability to select those in which you desire to continuously entertain.

Here is where you recognize the true importance of "grounding yourself".

#333

The Leaders of the New Earth
by Le'Vell Zimmerman

It's in taking responsibility for the temporary emotions that you can truly heal, transmute and release them.

This is where you elevate beyond victimization.

You desired to expand your capacity of unconditional love based on your depth of empathy.

All are doing the absolute best that they can, including you beloved.

Know that you designed emotionally heavy experiences for yourself where in many cases you would have to forgive what would seem to be not your fault and "unforgivable" as a demonstration of your power beyond the illusions of this hologram.

Your example is serving countless souls in their own healing path of empathy and compassion beyond such distortions.

This is where you truly are The Leaders of the New Earth.

#333

Author page--

Cheryl Lunar Wind lives in the Mount Shasta area in a little town called Weed. She is a practicer of Mayan cosmology, Lakota ceremony, Star Knowledge and the Universal Laws including the Law of One. Her hobbies are writing poetry, music, dance, drum circles and love for all life; plant, animal and crystal. Cheryl has been a guide and spiritual teacher for many years. Now she shares wit and wisdom through poetry, and has published poetry books; Know Your Way, We Are One, Follow the White Rabbit, Love Your Light, LIFE: Shared thru Poetry, Come to Mount Shasta: Sacred Path Poetry, We Are Light, Finding Our Way Home, We Are Forever, Handshake With the Divine, Grand Rising: A New Day Has Dawned and Star Messages: Codes to Sing, Dance and Live by.

Testimonials---

"Cheryl's poetry is very inspiring--particularly the way she compares life with the forces of nature. There is a special element in her poems that opens my heart and fills my soul with divine possibilities."
Giovanna Taormina, Co-Founder, One Circle Foundation

"Cheryl's poems have helped me to uncover and honor my own hidden memories. The beauty of her spirit is evident in each tender, insightful passage."
Marguerite Lorimer, www.earthalive.com

"A rare collection filled with raw, courageous honesty. Thought provoking words that will stop you in your tracks."
Snow Thorner, ED Open Sky Gallery, Montague, California

"When wisdom, guidance, confirming comfort, ect. arrives to us humans--from beings with the perspective of other realms--it is a divine gift. Especially in the form of what we call poetry, and through a being with no agenda; Cheryl Lunar Wind simply shares what source gives her!"
--Dragon Love (Thomas) Budde

Cheryl,
Greetings and Happy Monday to you my friend. I just
wanted to share with you that every time I read
'Come to Mount Shasta', even now that I'm mentioning
it I cry, I cannot help it, it is such a Divine message and
so impeccable in its timing. I came up here for Spirit, you
know I was called by Source and I live on the mountain
and I just want to thank you. Your poem found me last
summer at the headwaters during the Alien and Angels
conference; and then I found your book sitting in the
gazebo and I just can't stop, I love it! I love you, thank you.
---Jim

Cheryl,
Just want to thank you for your bringing me into the community
at Shasta. What you are doing/did do is absolutely changing
my life. You did it, you were instrumental in helping me set
my true path. Spirit is moving and the more of us that listen
and act the sooner the shift will be completed.
---Darrel

About Cheryl's poetry--
"You are dynamic! I have known no one who does so much so
swiftly, and your writing touches my heart because it comes
from your heart."
---The Durwood Show

"Your words are my words. I keep your book 'Know Your Way'
on my nightstand. I read it at bedtime and morning."
---Karina Arroyo

"Cheryl's words work magic in my heart, stirring the wisdom
that is buried so deeply within me---beautiful indeed!"
---Ellie Pfeiffer, founder of Ellie's Espresso & Bakery, Weed, CA

www.ingramcontent.com/pod-product-compliance
Lightning Source LLC
Chambersburg PA
CBHW071744020426
42331CB00008B/2160